T0099596

DIRT ROAD HOME

POEMS BY
CHERYL SAVAGEAU

CURBSTONE PRESS

Some of these poems have appeared or will appear in the following periodicals and anthologies:
Ad Hoc Monadnock, AGNI, An Ear To The Ground, The Boston Review, Durable Breath, The Eagle, The Indiana Review, The Little Apple, The Lobe, Massachusetts Review, The Nebraska English Journal, Poetry Like Bread, Reinventing The Enemy's Language, Returning the Gift, River Styx, SAIL, Sojourner, Two Worlds Walking, and The Worcester Review.

Many of the poems originally appeared in Home Country, Alice James Books, 1992.

FIRST EDITION, 1995; 2nd printing 2006.
Copyright © 1995 by Cheryl Savageau
All Rights Reserved

Printed in the U.S. on acid-free paper by BookCrafters
Cover design: Les Kanturek

Curbstone Press is a 501(c)(3) nonprofit publishing house whose operations are supported in part by private donations and by grants from governemt agencies, and foundations.

Library of Congress Cataloging-in-Publication Data

Savageau, Cheryl, 1950-
    Dirt road home / by Cheryl Savageau.
        p.   cm.
    ISBN 1-880684-30-6
    I. Title.
PS3569.A836D5 1995
811'.54--dc20   94-23647

published by
CURBSTONE PRESS   321 Jackson Street   Willimantic, CT 06226

In memory of my father,
Paul Joseph Savageau, Sr.
(1923-1986)
and for my mother,
Cecile Savageau Hall

Author's Acknowledgements

Special thanks to the many people who have supported me during the writing of these poems: to Joseph Bruchac and Martín Espada for their generous encouragement; to Katherine Gilbert-Espada, Adelle Leiblein, Marie Louise St. Onge, and Natasha Tretheway for helpful suggestions; to Miriam Goodman for getting me started; to Sam Cornish for encouragement at a time when I needed it; to the people at the National Endowment for the Arts and the Massachusetts Artists Foundation for Fellowships in Poetry—I cannot say enough thanks for the time the awards gave me, as well as the gift of saying this work is important; to the MacDowell Colony, many thanks for the luxury of a beautiful studio and uninterrupted work time for the first time in my life; to Doris Seale for her strength of spirit; to Carlyn Ekstrom for encouragement, hospitality and pep talks; to all my friends and family for their continual support and their belief in the importance of stories; to Inez Peterson, Loida Maritza Pérez, Elizabeth Graver and Steve Kuusisto for long talks and careful listening; special thanks to David Williams for invaluable help with the manuscript; and especially to Bill Siegel, partner and companion, in poetry and life.

CONTENTS

Sometimes The Dirt Road
Is The Only Way To Get There

Coming home, in this land we now call America, is one of the hardest things any contemporary poet can do. Perhaps that is why so many contemporary books of poetry concentrate on charting—with infinite detail and craft—interior labyrinthine landscapes which bear little relation to external reality. Coming home is not easy. It is even harder when that homeland is no longer on any maps but kept in the memory of yourself and those few others who see beyond the roadsigns and beneath the concrete. Here, where there is now something called New England, not so long ago there was only Ndakinna, "Our Land." Not gone, but hard for some people to find. And sometimes, as my grandfather used to say to me, "the only way to get there is to take the dirt road."

Like *Home Country*, Cheryl Savageau's first book whose poems make up the heart of this new volume, *Dirt Road Home* is a chronicle of returning. It is a return which takes her back to her family on both her mother's and her father's sides and a returning to a land which never abandoned her. She does this again and again in such poems as "Survival," even though, as is the case with most "Americans" of mixed ancestry, her Native vision of that land has been called into question throughout her life, diminished, and distorted by virtually every institution—political, religious, social, or medical—meant to maintain her and to shape her into a "healthy and educated citizen." Her family and the earth have helped her see in another way and find that back road which leads straight to the heart.

In a very real sense, "seeing," the physical act of vision which becomes a spiritual experience, is at the center of her poems. The brief poem "Genealogy" plays with her grandmother's family name "Lafford" to shape that kind of necessary double vision:

> Her maiden name
> she always told me was
> Laforte, the strong,
> but now i find it is Lafford,

as in a place to cross rivers
as in having to pay the price
of crossing.

Then there is the poem for her father, "Trees" which contains these sight-shaping lines:

You taught me the land so well
that all through my childhood
I never saw the highway,
the truckstops, lumberyards,
the asphalt works,
but instead saw the hills,
the trees, the ponds on the south end
of Quinsigamond...

Instead of focusing on those highly visible elements of western civilization, the roads which cut the heart of the land, the garish signs of roadside commerce, the industries which have as the central purpose the destruction of forests and the covering of the earth with lifeless crust, her father taught her to see something older and infinitely more alive: "all New England a forest."

But Savageau does not view reality with either blind or selective eyes. In "Like the Trails of Ndakinna," a simple quote from her father gives us a glimpse of a complexity of experience which has to be recognized as one of the hidden mixed-blood truths of America:

We're French and Indian like the war
my father said
they fought together
against the English
and though that's true enough
it's still a lie
French and Indian
still fighting in my blood

That sort of vision is often painful, but it is needed now more than ever. Celebrations of the earth, not through the medium of a reborn "noble savage," but in the voice of a woman of this century who realizes that being part of this world, being heir to more than one blood, neither disenfranchises you from speaking for the land nor means that you must spend a lifetime mourning what you and the world might have been without Europeans, are vitally needed today.

Savageau's poems do display care and craft—she is a poet who obviously knows the virtue of hard-won clarity—and her subject matter is not limited to explorations of her Abenaki ancestry. Her voice, though, is that of a storyteller and one can only tell stories well when one has listened to stories for a long time. Then those stories shape every word you speak. They may be old stories of the earth or new stories such as the eloquently understated prose poem "At the A&W" in which, after the young narrator reads from the Vermont guidebook that "No Indians ever lived within the state of Vermont..." her father responds "Those Indians sure were smart...they knew just where those borders were going to be."

It is no accident that the last poem in this book was also the final piece in her first collection. It gives us the image of a woman who is both Savageau herself and all women who are close to Native understanding of their real and mythical place on this earth." (By "Native," in this case, I mean one who knows the nature of the land which gave her birth, one who acknowledges the blood which makes her human— be it African blood or Asian, European, or American Indian.) In "All Night She Dreams," the narrator sees the powerful animals of the three directions in old stories—the panther west wind, the north wind bear, the moose which is the wind of the east. She feels herself on the back of the great turtle which holds the earth and then, like the first woman to be born and to die on earth, she dreams herself returning to the land. From her grave will sprout the squash and beans and corn. But until then, her breath—and the poems which ride on that breath, a breath which joins with the winds of Ndakinna, will rise:

> like smoke, like mist
> like welcome clouds
> like some green and beautiful plant.

—Joseph Bruchac
November 1994 / Frost Moon

DIRT ROAD HOME

Henri Toussaints

When Henri Toussaints
came down from Quebec
his hands already knew
the fine shape of the world
the hungry feel of earth
eager to be sown
the wet hard flank of a mare
the proper curve of a cradleboard.

His hands had eased the young
from sheep and mares
had freed the bound egg
and women
with no doctor about
with the pains coming close
wanted his hands
to navigate the maze
to bring the child
to first light.

Later the husbands would say
come, Henri, to dinner
eat with us, Henri
and they would sit to table
for the coming of new life
demands great things.

Later, much later,
Rosa had cried out
on the marriage bed
and the blood had come
red and strong and not stopping
as if getting were as hard as birthing.
He had soothed her then as if
she were one of his fine
mares, had crooned
Rosa, ma pauvre, Rosa, ma poule,
til she had quieted
and the bleeding stopped.

She brought him his first son
head so small it barely filled his palm
too small to live, they told him
but in the box behind the stove
next to the steaming kettle
and with Rosa's good milk
the boy had thrived.

Still, when Henri held him
he sang Il p'tit, Rosa, he's small,
and so they called him,
though his name was Armand
and he grew to be a man large
of hand and chest,
still they called him Ipsy
from his father.

And others followed:
Marie, called Tootsie, all small,
Eva, 'tipoule, little chicken,
and Peter who was called Bébé,
though there were more born after him,
eight in all, and Baby Alice,
who was born with red curls
and a hole in her heart.

Cold spring nights
the hole grew grave-size
settled in his own heart
mocked his healer's hands.

In the kitchen at night
with the oil lamp burning
he placed the fine gears
into the ancient watch.

The priests are wrong, Rosa,
it is not in the heart
that the soul lives,
but here,
in the hands.

Grandmother

Grandmother, you don't know me
but they say I walk as you did,
in touch with the earth.

Grandmother, when you met him
did you unbraid your hair?
Nobody will tell me, Grandmother,
what happened to your hair.

You bore him fine white babies, Grandmother,
their cheekbones high, eyes black,
noses never quite European.

Did you love him, Grandmother,
this white man, this cutter
of trees?

He was a strong man, they say,
walked over half the continent,
lived to be two weeks short of a hundred.
He's legend in these parts.

Grandmother, why
are there no stories
about you?
Grandmother, nobody will tell me
what happened to your hair.

When I was a child, Grandmother,
the earth was my body
and I played in the rain
happy as a frog.
And Grandmother, the hurricane
was my raindance
and the trees
sheltered me

and the sun, the sun
made my body
as red as yours, Grandmother,
as brown as yours.

Grandmother, they knew about you.
And Grandmother, they told me my eyes
are blue.
And Grandmother, they wouldn't tell me
your name.
Grandmother, Grandmother,
I was singing to you,
and they cut off
my hair.

Trees

—for my father, Paul J. Savageau, Sr.

You taught me the land so well
that all through my childhood
I never saw the highway,
the truckstops, lumberyards,
the asphalt works,
but instead saw the hills,
the trees, the ponds on the south end
of Quinsigamond that twined
through the tangled underbrush
where old cars rusted back to earth,
and rubber tires made homes for fish.

Driving down the dirt road home,
it was the trees you saw first,
all New England a forest.
I have seen you get out of a car,
breathe in the sky, the green
of summer maples, listen for the talk
of birds and squirrels, the murmur
of earthworms beneath your feet.
When you looked toward the house,
you had to shift focus,
as if it were something
difficult to see.

Trees filled the yard
until Ma complained,
where is the sun.
Now you are gone,
she is cutting them down
to fill the front with azaleas.

The white birch you loved,
we love. Its daughters
are filling the back.
Your grandchildren play
among them. We have taught them

as you taught us, to leave
the peeling bark, to lean
their cheeks against
the powdery white and hear
the heartbeat of the tree.
Sacred, beautiful, companion.

Looking For Indians

My head filled with tv images
of cowboys, warbonnets and renegades,
I ask my father
what kind of Indian are we, anyway.
I want to hear Cheyenne, Apache, Sioux,
words I know from television
but he says instead
Abenaki. I think he says Abernathy
like the man in the comic strip
and I know that's not Indian.

I follow behind him
in the garden
trying to step in his exact footprints,
stretching my stride to his.
His back is brown in the sun
and sweaty. My skin is brown
too, today, deep in midsummer,
but never as brown as his.

I follow behind him like this
from May to September
dropping seeds in the ground,
watering the tender shoots
tasting the first tomatoes,
plunging my arm, as he does,
deep into the mounded earth
beneath the purple-flowered plants
to feel for potatoes
big enough to eat.

I sit inside the bean teepee
and pick the smallest ones
to munch on. He tests
the corn for ripeness
with a fingernail, its dried silk
the color of my mother's hair.
We watch the winter squash grow hips.

This is what we do together
in summer, besides the fishing
that fills our plates unfailingly
when money is short.

One night
my father brings in a book.
See, he says, Abenaki,
and shows me the map
here and here and here
he says, all this
is Abenaki country.
I remember asking him
what did they do
these grandparents
and my disappointment
when he said no buffalo
roamed the thick new england forest
they hunted deer in winter
sometimes moose, but mostly
they were farmers
and fishermen.

I didn't want to talk about it.
Each night my father
came home from the factory
to plant and gather,
to cast the line out
over the dark evening pond,
with me, walking behind him,
looking for Indians.

Ol' Crazy Baker

We thought it was fun
ridin' our bicycles past the cottage
where Ol' Crazy Baker lived.
We pedaled downhill
as hard as we could
then coasted by
our hands on our heads yellin'
Hey, Mrs. Baker, Mrs. Baker...

She never disappointed us.
Even in winter
she'd be out with a hose
spraying the walk in her
yellow cloth coat
and white rubber boots.
Ol' Baker always wore yellow.
All summer long a yellow
sundress
with her skinny freckled legs
stickin' out
and a big yellow sunbonnet.
Ol' Baker was crazy for yellow.
Even her sneakers, yellow.
Crazy Ol' Baker.

Crazy Ol' Baker,
she'd spray anyone with that hose.
I remember even grownups
drivin by in convertibles
the radio up loud
and Ol' Baker'd be out with her hose
and let loose right at them.

I remember my father gettin' it
through the open window of the Chevy
once
and all us kids cheerin'
that Crazy Ol' Baker lady

and my father cussin'
about that crazy ol' bitch
and my mother hushin' him
and sayin' it wasn't her fault.

That last summer I remember
Ol' Crazy Baker came out
without her sunbonnet
and without her yellow sneakers
and with her sundress over
her head
and we all stood around laughin'
at Ol' Crazy Baker's
new stunts
til she began to shout
Come on then and get it, Harry,
you bastard,
and policemen came
and stood around
snickerin'
and not lookin'
at Ol' Crazy Baker
flappin' around loose like that
and her skinny legs all
freckled
and Ol' Baker yellin' at them
You're all bastards, Harry, they're all
everyone bastards
and she danced around in her loose
flesh
til I remember my mother came
and said to her
Come into the house now
Lillian

At the Fireworks

The hill is thick with people we don't know,
but feel like we do. My mother lays out a blanket,
and we are sitting in the grass at Greenhill Park,
or standing in the rivers of dark between families,
swirling our sparklers, careful not to send sparks
onto surrounding blankets.

A voice comes over the loudspeaker,
and my father searches his pockets for matches,
finds one and lights it. Look, my mother says.
Around us tiny flames appear all over the hill.
We are part of a circle of light, small fires
in the dark, fireflies, and the silent agreement
of heat lightning sporadically in the clouds.

As the music begins, my father's voice comes
from that place inside where the war never stopped,
If they dropped a bomb on Worcester,
he says, *this would be the time and place.*

When the sky erupts in blossoms
of red, white, blue, silver, green, gold,
my father's words won't stop ringing
in that hollow place in my stomach that
the noise touches and the earth pulls.

The finale begins, the familiar notes,
and the blossoms change,
become *bombs bursting in air,*
that terrible song.

The booming goes on,
the whistles and cracks,
the sky full of unwelcome light.
We sit, vulnerable on a hillside,
silent, among strangers.

Gifts

—for my parents

I spend all my paper route money
on presents for cousins and grandparents,
then make gifts from whatever I can find,
cut up old Christmas cards to make new ones,
search through my stuff for things
that might make someone smile.

I add them to the pile
that grows beneath the tree,
where everything we need for the year
is wrapped in colored paper—
underwear, socks, toothbrushes,
mixed in with the toys and books and winter boots.

My parents go in debt each year for this.
My mother's sisters shake their heads
and blame it on my father's folly,
their husbands call him crazy
the year he's out of work and gifts
still pile up under the tree
what does he think he is, rich?

And it is true, they are rich,
my mother and father both,
as the world flows through their hands,
as they give and give, like Santa
who is, my parents tell me,
a spirit as real as the snow
that follows him from the North.
Where else does this winter harvest come from?

Everything is a gift,
there is no such thing as necessity.
Even the air we breathe, the sunlight,
this mysterious music of breath and heartbeat,
hand touching hand, the words
we say to each other in deep night,
this life received and given back.

Just His Eyes

It's because I wear glasses
he explains to me
on the bleachers at the little league field
where neither of us plays
he tells me this story
about the boys club
how the kids there called him Chink
how he told them over and over
no, I'm French, I'm French
as they pushed him beneath
the water, held him down
Chink, Chink.

They thought I was Chinese
he explains to me
his little cousin, a girl,
and safe to tell secrets to,
but it's because
there's something wrong
with my eyes

Five years younger than he is
I try hard to see what's wrong with his eyes
but they are just his eyes, black as his hair,
not blue like mine, or green like his sister's

If he'd known enough
to be able to tell the truth
about his eyes
he might have heard Tonto,
dirty Indian, savage,
but we were French
and there was something
wrong
with his eyes

Now it's his eyes I see
when he says *who cares*
if some grandfather
slept with a squaw
It's his eyes I speak to
when I say
that squaw
was your grandmother

What I do not wear on my face
I wear in my heart
I want to hear him say
there's nothing wrong with his eyes
I want to hear him say
grandmother

What the Boy Said

Everytime we go on a long drive
my father starts singing
Indian songs
my mother tells him stop
please, she says, you can't sing

after a while
he switches to sad
country songs
that's when I say, Dad, please
you can't sing

At the A & W

It is 1960, and we are on the way to Uncle Phil's new house. We have a new car, a really new car for the first time, my father having a good job this year, my mother expecting a fifth child. This is one of the good years, my dad not laid off. It is a station wagon, sea blue, with three seats, the way-back seat facing backwards. Next year my mother will be hit by a car going through an intersection, and will die for a little while. She will float on the ceiling, watching the doctors work on her, calling out to each other in medical shorthand that her pressure is dropping, they don't have a pulse, and she'll want to tell them not to worry, she's quite all right. She and the baby she now carries will spend the winter with broken collar bones, she in a cast from neck to waist, the baby in a figure eight bandage. Now all the seats are down so we can stretch out and be comfortable. My father has put furniture pads and pillows in the back. I am the oldest, and I'm reading aloud from the Vermont guidebook. No Indians ever lived within the state of Vermont, I read to whoever might be listening. This reading is already a passion. At this time of my life, I read whatever has words on it, I am not selective. Those Indians sure were smart, my father says, they knew just where those borders were going to be. I am not sure what he means but laugh with him, anyway. As we leave Massachusetts he has me looking for the state line. Quick before you miss it, he says. From the back window all I see is the highway cutting through endless trees. The road is winding out behind us and I am straining to see something different. Can't you see it? he calls back to me and I have to tell him no it's just the same, trees, road, then suddenly I see a hawk flying overhead. Look, Dad, a redtail, I tell him, and we are watching together, my father leaning forward over the steering wheel, my mother pointing for the baby, my sister and brothers kneeling on the back seat to look up at the hawk circling above our heads. Later on, my father will take my baby brother to the bathroom of an A&W rootbeer place, where we actually *buy* hamburgers, fries, and rootbeer in frosted mugs, and he will come out to the car to look for reading material. He can't go, he needs something to read, he tells my mother. There are no picture books in the car. I offer my book, but my father says it's no good, he needs pictures. The only possibility is the map, which my father takes back with him. My brother studies the map in the bathroom of an A&W, my father showing him the road we're on, the rivers and lakes, cities and towns, and eventually my brother has success and they return to the car. This is a story my father will tell over and over again, how his two year old had to have something to read in the john of an A&W.

Thorns

You jump in religious ecstasy
on Memere's bed
and I jump beside you
staring at the twin hearts
floating against the blue sky
one circled by thorns
the other by roses

They're bleeding
you screech in my ear
in mid-jump
I am watching you
not the hearts
I sleep under every night
No they're not, I say
Yes, look, they're bleeding, you insist
your face flushed and sweaty
eyes wide, arms rising and falling
as you jump and stare
I struggle to see what you see
and almost I see them shimmer against
the sky, the red drops glistening

Now when I see your mother
at family weddings
I ask her about you,
how you're doing
Not so good she tells me
the doctors say
she's one of those
depressed maniacs

It's your mother who had fallen
under the hands of the priests
slain in the spirit

*Memere—pronounced Mem-ay. French-Canadian for
"Gramma." The "r" is not sounded.*

she lay on the wooden floor,
surrounded by shadows ululating
like babies hypnotized by their own voices

I remember you told me
how you walked the freeway in california
to get milk for your baby
no store for five miles, no car,
your husband out on a binge
how you agonized
whether to take the baby with you
finally left him in his crib
and came home to find a house
full of men—your husband
and his friends who all wanted food
and a friendly fuck
I don't remember how you escaped
their groping hands and leering
alcohol mouths, or if you did
I blot it out
but I remember how your brother
threw you down a flight of stairs,
angry that you tried to leave
his drinking buddy,
the man who beat you
You worried aloud for the next four months
that the baby you carried would be an idiot
damaged irreversibly

Gloria, you always were a maniac,
dying your hair green in seventh grade
for St. Patrick's day
We're not even Irish
I told you, watching in disbelief
fascinated by your daring

You pushed needles through my ears
barely numbed with ice cubes
the only time I was brave enough
to follow your lead with no holding back,
and you caught me as I fainted,
spilling rubbing alcohol across the table and floor,

my little sister running outside to tattle
to returning parents
We laughed all night under blankets

Now I hear of you through family gossip
the lost jobs, suicide attempts, hospitalizations,
the latest man doing you wrong, the saintliness
of your mother taking you in

You told me the heart with roses is Mary
the one with thorns, Christ
but I know they are both you, Gloria,
a heart where roses bloomed
surrounded by thorns

Harsh Words

1.

Auntie Blanche is visiting and I am making myself invisible so I can stay
and not be sent out to watch a baby or pitch balls to my little brother.
My mother is entertaining in the parlour, not in the kitchen. She is
bringing in coffee and tea. The milk is in a pitcher, the sugar in a bowl.
She has made pie and brownies, which she hands to me to pass around.
I am waiting, because I know it will happen, and it does. As my mother
walks in, her red hair curling around her face and over her shoulders,
the words I've dreaded come and I can't stop them. *Why don't you cut
your goddam hair?* My Aunt bites into the words that bite into my
mother's smile. In front of me, my mother grows smaller. I have stayed
to defend her. I want to spill the coffee, milk, any distracting thing, but I
am too much her daughter to do it. Auntie Blanche sits, her own red
hair gone yellow grey, waiting for an answer. I push the plate of brownies
in front of her. *Would you like one?* I ask politely.

2.

I'll admit it, I was afraid of her harsh words. Now I knit sweaters of my
own design, love the loft of the yarn, the rich and subtle colors of wool.
But then, my fingers clumsy, she declared me book smart. *Can't do
anything useful,* she said, taking the needles from my fumbling grasp.
For years I hid my shameful hands.

I could play piano, but not so well as Rita, diaper a baby, but not like my
mother could, cook, but never as well as Memere, never got anything
clean enough, couldn't throw a ball or draw a line straight. My hands
sought out the curves and textures of life, held still for the visit of a
dragonfly, caressed the downy backs of bees.

I didn't know then the story I would find out later, how she fought for
my mother to finish high school, working long hours to make up the
difference. How she vowed to never marry, then, surprised by passion,
married a man who loved the bottle. *I went crazy for a little while,* she
told me, *and married a man I didn't need.*

21

3.

He was the uncle who scared me, who drove down our dirt road cursing the mud, ridges, or dust depending on the season, picking up my grandmother for dinner, then gunning it and afterward complaining of the muffler or shocks ruined by the sunofabitchin road. It wasn't the road he hated, but us, my mother's beauty, my father's calm determination and the books next to his chair. He thought we felt we were too good for him, but it was he who thought that, the lack of beer in our refrigerator a constant recrimination. He kept his distance, and kept my aunt, who did not drive, away from family, ridiculed the driving lessons that could have meant her freedom, until she quit under his harsh words, and then he criticized her for that. Some Sundays she called her mother, invited her for dinner, and then he must drive, cursing the trees, his wife, the road, this world he couldn't love and knew, for sure, didn't love him.

4.

I was a damn good cook, she told my mother in the weeks before her death. *Yes, Blanche, you were a terrific cook.* My mother is feeding her lunch. *Why couldn't he tell me that. He'd never tell me that. I'm eating it, aren't I? That's all he'd say.*

He was weak, my mother says. Blanche sees her husband's girth and weight, his very presence a pout, a sneer. *Yes,* she says, *he was weak.*

5.

He thought I was a bad example, my mother tells me. *Too free,* he said. *He never learned what your Daddy knew, you get more flies with honey than with vinegar.*

6.

I meet her daughter at the hospital. She tells me she took her mother some mashed potatoes for supper. *You know how she loves her mashed potatoes,* she says. I mention how comforting that must have been, how she must have enjoyed that. *Oh, no,* Janet tells me. *She says to me, What's the matter, don't you know how to cook a damned potato?* I picture her as she eats the warm and buttery meal, grumbling, *Not enough salt.*

7.

What is it I want to tell you about the love between sisters, mothers, aunts and daughters? About the life of a woman who went crazy and paid, about the harsh words we send out to protect our own hearts, that turn on us, and imbed themselves like the quills of a porcupine, seeking the vital organs?

8.

All week long my grandmother haunts me. She is here, at my elbow, standing behind me as I work, watching me as I eat. She comes always in times of trouble, but I am fine, my husband well, my son happy in his work. She will not talk to me. *She's here,* I tell my husband. *But it's not about me.*

So we are not surprised to get the news. I tell my sister that Memere was nearby all week. Blanche was calling for her, that's what the nurses said. She was calling for her mother. My sister says what we both know. *Memere was already there,* she tells me.

Glissandos

Aunt Louise's screened-in summer house is the place we like best to sit, my sister and I, watching the boats out on the lake, swinging on the porch swing that has soft pillows and creaks gently. Next to the swing is a stack of *Playboy* magazines that my mother doesn't know is there. We think it's funny that Uncle Raymond buys these magazines full of naked women, funny that they even exist. But nevertheless, we turn the pages, looking at one woman after another, as we push the floor with our feet, swinging harder, lying back on pillows as we giggle and point. We think of Aunt Louise, way older than my mother and barrel-shaped, her Sunday dress and wide-brimmed hats, her voice a glissando over the high notes of the hymns. She would never be in one of these magazines, she is tight-lipped angry when she finds us with the pile of them open around us, our skin flushed from swinging and looking, but later I hear family stories about a party long ago, a few too many drinks, and Aunt Louise's breasts set free from her tight brassiere, swinging, round, loose and perfect, glistening with sweat, glissandos of motion to the tinkling piano's ragtime beat.

French Girls Are Fast

French girls are fast
I find this out
before I know what it means
Two days in the Irish-Catholic school
my mother thought would keep me safe from sin
and the name is following me around.
Frenchie, hey, Frenchie,
ooh la la
the Irish boys leer
staring at the roundness
I am not ashamed of
the Irish girls still properly flat
beneath their uniform jackets

I learn quickly to sneer
light my cigarette with a wooden match
flicked against the brick school wall
taste the smoke, roll it over my tongue
and exhale upward in a gesture
of exquisite boredom
I tighten my face, turn
to look them up and down
and spit out the prayer
of this place—
eat it, assholes

Years later it is a grandmother
who accuses me
and I hear it again
French girls are fast
who am I to say otherwise
my belly pushing outward
with her grandson's child

She admonishes me
not to rest my hands on my belly
You'll ruin the baby
touching yourself like that...

My hands fly away for a moment
like frightened birds
looking for another place to perch
then settle back down
She shrugs and turns away

Later she digs out a blanket
she bought at Niagara Falls
from those Indians, you know,
she tells me, shaking her head,
clicking her tongue
but the blanket is nice, she says,
you can use it

I will not tell her now
my father's family is Indian,
that the blood was mixed in me
generations ago
My hands accept the white wool,
finger the stripes
of red, yellow, black, green
I draw it over me, the child,
my unruly hands, feel my body slowing,
getting ready for the long push ahead

Card Shark

—for Inez

I know the feel
of his hands on me
his caresses
as he riffles through me
parting my members
dealing me in
spreading me like a fan
his senses keen
noting my every possibility
every possible trick.
He peruses the kitty
choosing carefully
until finally
everything fits
and with a grunt
of satisfaction
he goes out.

Barbie

i. *The Discovery*

It is true she has
perfect bladder control.
But she suspects something
is missing.
Fingers slide over her crotch
and she begins to feel
a fullness, a budding,
a turning inward.
She dreams of caves,
of thickets and thorns,
dark mouths in the night.
Moths flutter inside her.
She wants to split her skin.
She wants to blossom like a rose.
She wants bees to crawl over her,
probing and sucking in the hot sun.
She wants to be the lush wet
forest floor.
She wants to carry the bowl of the sky.

ii. *She Worries About Her Hips*

Her hips have begun to spread,
there's no denying it.
Now that she's taught her legs to bend,
to open wide in the night,
her buttocks have built a firmer cushion.
Her jeans no longer fit.
Her thighs grow strong.
At the dark of the moon,
they are covered with blood.

iii. *Her Hair*

Short, long. Blond, red,
black, brown. All her life
she's sat with a bubble on her head
in rollers, rags, pins,
with lotions and creams that stung
her scalp, and sprays
that made it hard to breathe.
One day, she shaves it all off.
Lank or bushy, streaked with grey,
what grows back will be hers.

iv. *Her Feet*

Her grandmother warned her about shoes.
How the muscles would change,
the back ache. Now her feet
want to walk on tiptoe forever.
She forces her heels to the floor,
lets them hang over the backs of stairs.
She will learn to walk again,
letting the whole length of her foot
feel the ground. Feel
the heel touch, the toes grasp
the luxurious roll forward.
She will learn to run.

Like A Good Joke: Grandma at Ninety

—for my grandmother, Delia Lafford Savageau

I have carried her swollen leg
around with me all day.
For seven and a half weeks
she has hidden this,
walking up and down the corridor
sixteen, seventeen, eighteen times,
no blame wheelchair for her.
She lives alone, the doctors whisper.
Last night the swelling became too great.

I have come prepared to mourn,
but she is laughing.
It's not a clot, she grins.
I've got them stumped.
She is proud of this,
her body's resistance
to their probing.
And don't tell them anything,
she says. They'll cut
my blame leg off.

When a bell rings in the hall
I hear myself asking
what's that for?
Maybe someone died, she says
rolling her eyes. She rocks
back and forth, laughing, watching
my face. Or else it's the ice cream man.

I see her disappearing,
her rocking chair edging
toward a cliff she can't see,
but she stops my look—

Enjoy life, my girl, it's so short.
She shakes her head, then giggles again.
Only not for me, she says,
and smacks the arms of her chair
with glee. She carries her
ninety years like a good joke.

My little doctor, she says,
I asked him, Doctor,
how am I made?
Damn good, he told me, damn good.

Leah

When after days of labor
trying to push the baby out
the doctor told Frank
I can't save them both,
how lucky for you
that Frank didn't know
what the priests would've said
and told the doctor simply
save my wife.

I think of you now, Leah,
great-aunt, Grandma's littlest sister,
sitting primly on the high-back chair
in the new dress she'd made for you,
bow in your hair, stockings
pulled up to your knees,
high brown shoes laced tight.

Three times you tried
and each time lost
the baby you'd carried
full term, a doctor's blunder
not once, but two times,
and then the third birth,
a baby so perfect, you said,
so beautiful, he lived ten days
without a rectum.

I know you as the fat aunt
who still cooks cabbage for her Polish husband
dead thirty years, a good cop killed
by punks, you tell me, an honest cop,
as if I doubt you.

In every room television light
rainbows your face
through colored cellophane
you've taped to the screens.

As cancer laces your body tighter
and you grow every day smaller
your bath is littered with tabloids,
tea-bag fortunes are taped to your doors.
There is nothing too bizarre
to be believed or hoped.

First Grade—Standing In the Hall

—for my brother, Ed Savageau

Because he can't read
the teacher makes him stand
in the hall. He can sing
all his letters, knows
what they look like. He knows
that out of books come stories,
like the ones his Gramma told him.
Now she is in the hospital.
He wonders if she is sleeping,
when she will come home.

The letters do not
talk to him.
They keep their stories
to themselves.

He is hopeless, he is stupid,
he is standing in the hall.
He is waiting in the hall
for the principal
to see him, for the bell to ring,
for the teacher
to call him back inside.

After awhile
when no one comes
he stops crying.
A spider is webbing
the pie-shaped window pane
and outside,
the sun is making fire
in the yellow leaves.

If he listens closely
a song will begin in him
that the teachers
can't silence.

Hanging Clothes In the Sun

—for my brother, Ed Savageau

His youngest daughter helps him
wring the clothes
while his wife answers phones
for doctors. The washing machine
is broken again.

In the factory
where he etches pathways
onto silicon chips
he wears a white coat and pants,
special shoes
to protect the chips from dust.

This is the best job he's had.
Better than last year
when he sprayed lawns with poisons,
then set up little signs
warning others not to walk there,
his clothes saturated,
his asthmatic lungs
choking on the clouds
marked hazardous to pets and humans.

All summer, he'd had to refuse
his daughters' hugs until
he removed his poisonous clothes
on the back stoop. Tee shirt,
jeans, baseball cap,
he put them in a plastic bag,
and showered while his skin burned.

Before that it was asbestos.
Wrapped in plastic,
he'd removed the sagging ceilings,
the flaking insulation on basement pipes,
vacuuming to remove the tiny particles
that would lodge in the lungs.

They floated in dreams, followed him
like a swarm of invisible bees.

This job was better than that,
in spite of the tanks of solvents
leaking noxious fumes,
the paychecks that didn't stretch.
Better than working at the defense plant
across the lake, where Air Force personnel
checked his I.D. badge each morning,
where everything and nothing was secret.

He squeezes water
out of shirts and towels.
He knows he drinks too much.
He dreams of moving to New Hampshire,
where his people walked
for 10,000 years,
and where, he believes,
the water is still clean,
but up north, the Lancaster paper mill
spills dioxin into the Connecticut River,
and downstream, five young girls have surgery
to remove cancerous wombs.
Anyway, there's no money.

Now the washing machine
is spewing soapy water
onto the basement floor.
His daughter frowns determinedly
at the towel in her hands.
At five years old, she knows how to help,
squeezing out the dirty water,
hanging clothes in the sun.

At Fifteen Louise Kills Chickens

—in memory of Louise Monfredo

When the order comes in
her mother is on her way to a sister's,
and her father is out haying.
Anyway, this is women's work.
You'll have to do it, Louise,
her mother said.
Forty chickens to the hotel before dinnertime.
Forty chickens plucked and dressed.

Louise holds the chicken in her arms
and swings its neck to the ground.
She places her boot firmly on the head
and pulls.

> It's the only way, she tells me sixty years later,
> to kill a lot of chickens in a hurry.

She tosses each bird
into the pot of boiling water
to loosen its feathers.
There's blood in the dust,
on her hands, her clothes,
red as her own blood that lately
she has welcomed as her body's secret promise.
But she is not thinking of that now.
She has to work quickly.
The sun is hot, and after the killing
there's more work to be done.

Plucking forty chickens takes time.
She works in a haze of feathers and blood
cleaning the insides, dropping
hearts, liver, and gizzard into one pile,
the waste into a waiting can.

> Could you do it by twisting their necks? I ask her.
> Oh, sure, if you're strong enough, she says.

As she works, time slips away.
It is just the crunch of the chickens' heads
under her boot, the slippery wet feathers,
the endless sorting and cleaning,
and the smell of blood and fowl.
She is making meat.

My grandmother told me she sang to them first, I say.
Is that possible? Louise laughs. Bet she
calmed them right down, she says.

When she looks up from the last of the birds
she wipes a hand across her forehead,
and squints at the horizon's thin line of grey.
She loads the wagon by herself, hitches the horses,
and goes inside to wash.

Louise delivers the chickens on time,
and remembers to collect what she is owed.
Forty chickens before dinnertime,
forty chickens plucked and dressed.
Her mother won't be disappointed.

And what came after that?
Did she make dinner for her mother's return?
Feed her father and brothers?
Did the sister die or live to bear more children?
Louise didn't say, but I do know this—
Afternoons, when the sky darkened
and blossomed grey
she slipped the saddle off her mare
and rode bareback
to meet the storm.

Logic Problem

the lesbians are on the third floor
the zippers for men's jeans are mainly on floor two
the directions for filing A.B. Dick are on floor one
the women who are easy lays are on floor two
the men are generally on floor one
the women who secretly agree they have no brains
are on the first floor
the women who are the hope of the world use colorful
language on the second floor
the woman reading Proust in the bathroom is on floor one
the woman who thinks she is a poet is on floor three
the woman who sings while she works is on the second floor
new leather bags are carried casually on floor three
the woman who has had three abortions is on floor three
the woman who had one abortion is no longer on floor two
the pictures of the Blessed Virgin are in lockers on the second floor
the pictures of naked women are in a locked desk on the first floor
Mother Jones is on the third floor
but she'd be more comfortable on the second

the woman who is unbuilding her life waits for directions
by the third floor phone
the man who calls in the night for his dead mother rings
for another cup of coffee on floor one
the woman with bruises blooming like roses on her breasts
waters the boss's plants on the ground floor
the man who secretly loves silk longs to visit the third floor
on the second floor the woman who has had four miscarriages
is taking codeine for menstrual distress
the woman whose son is learning to live without ecstasy
wears only natural fibers on the third floor

the woman on the first floor who is three months' pregnant visits the
bathroom to vomit her boss's smoke one more time
the woman whose husband did not come home last night
sneaks a cigarette in a second floor stairwell
on the ground floor, the woman whose mother is dying
enters the number '3' into the computer 400 separate times

the man whose wife is recovering from a mastectomy
is hunting for breast on floor two
the woman who dreams nightly of vaginal flowers
is not on the third floor

    in the harbor waters, luminous fish
    are circling
    what are their colors?

    when birds walk the parking lot
    in the grey off-shift hours,
    what is the quality of light?

    and the singing of stone
    that rings through the city—
    which of the women hears it?

Department of Labor Haiku

—for Martín Espada

In the winter snow
the kitchens fill up with steam
and men out of work

Why They Do It

Uncle Jack drinks because he's Indian.
Aunt Rita drinks
because she married a German.
Uncle Raymond drinks
because spats have gone out of style.
Uncle Bébé drinks
because Jeannie encourages him.
Aunt Jeannie drinks because Bébé does.
Russell drinks because he's in college.
Uncle Jack drinks
because he's a perfectionist.
Dave drinks because he's out of work.
Aunt Rita drinks
because she's a musician.
Bert drinks because he's married to Rita.
Renny drinks
because he likes a good time.
Gil drinks because he always has.
Raymond drinks
because Marie's too smart.
Jack drinks because Florence won't.
Lucille and Bob don't drink
because everyone else does.
Raymond drinks because of all the women
he'll never have.
Dick just drinks to empty the keg.

Bride

—for my mother, Cecile Meunier Savageau

My mother is the young bride
living with her husband's parents
she is forbidden to use the toaster
or touch the stove
After she uses the kitchen
careful not to drop a crumb
the floor is pointedly swept

This is the photo that doesn't exist
the one of my father and me alone
The sun is shining on my father's thin face
We are not outside a tenement stoop
but in front of someone's columned porch
I am wearing a dress with starched
and ironed ruffles

Somewhere off to the side
my mother stands by herself
not allowed into this shot
my grandmother wants
for the group on her chiffoniere

In this photo never taken
my mother will be imagined away
invisible as the Indians
my grandmother has expunged
from the family memory

My grandmother does not know yet
but maybe she guesses
the strength of this young woman
she should call daughter
but will not

Infant of Prague

My mother sews new clothes
for the Infant
who stands on the kitchen table
in his painted plaster robes.
These cold clothes are not enough.
His new robe will be red,
satin, lined with white,
and trimmed with metallic gold
rick-rack. Underneath,
he'll wear a long white dress,
embroidered with red and gold
crosses. More beautiful
than my brother's christening dress,
and shinier. She tries it on him,
warns me away,
this is not a doll, no toy
for me to dress and undress.
The infant stands
patiently
as she tries on the robe
and sews the scratchy lace
around his neck and wrists.
He doesn't fidget or cry
the way I do
when she fusses with my
hair and clothes. He is
a good child.

He holds a blue ball in his hands.
Ma tells me it is the world
but all I see is the sharp cross
growing out of the top, sure to
poke out an eye, cut
his pretty mouth when he falls.

Crêche

—for my brother, Paul Savageau

On a separate table
my mother sets up the crêche.
She pretends it is for us
but it is the mother she honors
her mother, herself,
and the Holy Mother,
the one she makes us pray to
all those long rosaries during Lent,

Hail Mary, full of grace,
blessed art thou amongst women
while the floor digs into my knees.
My sister and I get the giggles
when my brother prays diligently
hail Mary full of grace,
bless us while we're swimmin
Each repetition gets us going
and we can't stop. My mother says
nothing, her lips moving in prayer,
but later she tells us
my brother's prayers are good
even if he gets the words wrong.

She places the painted wooden figures
of Mary and Joseph, the Three Wise Men
and the Shepherds, but lets us place the animals,
the donkey, goats, sheep and camels.
She covers it all with angel hair, thick
as the webs of a thousand spiders
that catch the dazzling starlight
in that faraway land where there isn't any snow.

The Baby Jesus is there, surrounded
by warm animal breath. I wish
with all the babies my mother keeps having
she would have one at Christmas, our own winter child
blessed by all the animals, breathing the life of stars.

The Sound of My Mother Singing

—for my mother, Cecile Meunier Savageau

He drops a motor
on the dining room table,
bellows at the big girls.
Rita plays the piano
while Florence cries.
When he waves the butcher knife
in their mother's direction,
Eva pretends to faint
on the theory that no one
will hurt a sick person.

Outside, Bertha sneaks a smoke
under the stairs.
In the basement, Bébé holds
his pet rabbit inside his shirt.
There, he says, don't worry.
Pa won't hurt you.
He pets the silky fur,
feels the comfort of claws
and twitching nose against his chest.
Don't worry, don't worry.

Crouched behind the bedroom door,
Lucille, the youngest one, my mother,
watches through the crack.
Her mother moves silently
around the kitchen.
Her oldest sister, Marie,
puts food in front of her father,
fork, spoon, butterknife.
She pours coffee.
Slouched over his plate,
he has forgotten his rage,
forgotten the butcher knife,
and Marie slips it into a drawer.
Lucille watches him eat,
thick slices of cheese and onions,

a plate of steak and eggs.
Where is the redhead? he says,
looking up from his food.
Come, tête-rouge, he calls,
viens, viens.
He is speaking to her
from under his armpit,
head down, smiling
toward her hiding place.

She hears her mother speaking,
Stop, Henri, you frighten her.
But now he is waggling his fingers,
smiling at her. This
is her Pa's face.

Lucille sits on his lap
as he eats, it will be all right now,
he is smiling, he loves her,
his little tête-rouge,
she can make him smile.

Late in the night
she is awakened by Marie,
who carries her outside in her nightie.
Florence and Eva wait for them
behind the lilacs. Lucille
sees movement behind the shed
and waves to Bébé and Rita.
She likes this nighttime game
of hide and seek.

When Pa comes out of the house,
Lucille is wide awake. She leans forward
to call out to him. Here we are Pa,

she wants to say. She feels
Marie's hand over her mouth and remembers
not to talk.

In her father's hand the blade
reflects the moonlight.
Come out, les enfants, come out, he calls.
His voice is soft, cajoling
in the warm night.
Come out, children, come out, he croons,
so I can kill you.
    In the office
    Lucille types.
    She brings coffee, arranges calendars,
    cleans desks. She smiles often.
    Her boss calls her Red. She is the favorite.
    Soon she is calling banks, investing money
    for the company, forgetting it isn't her own.
    They tell her how good she is. She sings
    she flirts, she keeps them smiling.

Sing for me, tête-rouge,
her father says.
So she sings a song
he taught her
and he sings with her
that's right, that's right
sing some more
and she keeps on singing
while her mother cleans up
and her sisters watch.

        One day she is let go. No degree, they tell her.
        No one without a degree can do this job.

It is not clear
when the change comes,
when his hands become cruel
on her arms. He is saying over and over
You love your Pa? Hanh? You love your Pa?

She is crying. She has done something wrong.
She is trying but
she can't
sing
anymore.

What I Save

Like my grandmother now, I save teabags for a second cup. String, stamps
without postmarks, aluminum foil. Wrapping paper, paper bags, bags
of scrap fabric, blue rubber bands, clothes hangers. I save newspaper
clippings, recipes, bits of yarn, photographs in shoeboxes, tins of but-
tons. I save canceled checks, instruction manuals, warranties for appli-
ances long-since thrown away. Feathers, shells, pebbles, acorns. I save
faces, phrases, bits of melody, the light on the trees from a late autumn
day. I save my grandmother's hair, carefully braided and coiled in tissue
paper. I save the moment my infant son nuzzled my breast and began to
suck. I save my lover's hands touching me. I save his tongue, his teeth. I
save the strong smell of sex. I save the rhythm. I save the sound of geese
flying overhead, the smooth young bark against my cheek, the white
dust of birch on my hands.

I save the water flowing through me
that cannot be contained.

Equinox: The Goldfinch

it is as if he had swallowed the sun
which slept the winter inside him
until he forgot what it was like
to live in warmth, and golden.
but his body has the knack of timing.
for weeks now golden feathers
have appeared among the grey and khaki brown
now his back is mottled with ice floes
drifting in water that is not blue
but shining purest yellow

he rides upon the cusp of winter
and he is full of sun
it is too much for him to bear
his throat swells with it
and he pushes the sun out
into the air where it turns
immediately to song. The notes

fall back to him, and he tries again,
head back, throwing the sun
into the air, and it returns
to him, and yet again,
and again, there is no end
to this light that is filling him,
it is the sun he has become the sun.
his song shimmers with light
and his body blossoms
into yellow

Trickery: A May Poem

I.
Yesterday temperatures soared to 82,
until last night a cold front brought rain.
This morning I glance toward the window
and see white on the tree outside.
Snow again.

I make a quick breakfast,
refusing to open the blinds onto
more snow, no matter how
it follows the curve of the
branches, no matter that it will
melt away by noon, no matter
that in a month I will crave
its coolness against my skin.
Outside, birds are singing spring songs.

I sit head down at breakfast.
If I don't acknowledge it,
it will go away, but it's no use,
my eyes seek the space between
the curtains, the white that shouldn't
be there, it's spring after all,
and yes, I see the green behind the white.

This snow holds the branches oddly,
clustering around and between
the new leaves, and finally
I give in, the world does not
fit my expectations,
willed or not, I must see
this last snow. I pull back the curtains
onto a world of green. Outside the window—
appleblossoms.

II.
And now she is at it again.
The weight of winter snow
has split her three trunks
until they lie on the ground
around the heaving roots.
All winter we are amazed
at the symmetry of it—
the tree fallen like a blossom
on the back hill.

We stand in snow
that is thigh-deep, touching
the branches that had made fruit
too high for picking.

As the snow recedes
I watch downy woodpeckers
and nuthatches, their beaks
tracing the old bark to find niches
where grubs are waking to spring.

I think how they will miss her
once we've cut the limbs for firewood,
chipped the smaller branches into mulch
how she will feed us still, our fire
and gardens made the richer.

But ready to cut, we are stopped.
Against all reason, the sap
pushes the green buds
into growth once more.
We watch them swell
and wait in thanks for this last blessing—
from fallen wood,
appleblossoms.

Summer Solstice

For seven days I heard the cat
as she padded full-pawed
up the driveway,
crying steadily as she walked,
as if she were calling kittens
or a mate.

She stopped beneath the Japanese maple,
the place she'd chosen
to drop the tiny mouse
I hadn't seen she was carrying.

The mouse crouched in front of her
stunned or hypnotized,
and the cat looked around,
and began to sing.

Her voice rose and fell
in all the inflections known to cats.
The rolling tones that start deep in the throat
then open into invitation, the inquisitive hum
she'd used when nuzzling kittens, the demanding wail
I'd gotten used to hearing outside the kitchen door.

The mouse,
delicate-boned, velvet-furred,
never moved, never twitched
an ear or hair.

This went on for some time.
It was a very small mouse,
maybe born this spring
before the grasses bloomed.

I don't know how long exactly I watched,
but long enough for me to think
she doesn't really want the mouse,
long enough that in a fit

of human misunderstanding
I thought to save the mouse,
and walking toward them,
spoke the cat's name.

She looked up,
her eyes intent and distant,
then calmly picked up
the waiting mouse
and with one sure bite,
bit off its head and ate
bones and fur and all,
until there was nothing left
but a drop of blood
on her whiskery brow.

For seven days she did this
an hour or two before sunset
and after that first day I watched
from wherever the cry caught me,
surprised each time
by ceremony.

There is a love between hunter and prey
that I am just beginning to understand.

On the threshold of summer,
beneath the red-leafed tree,
she sang the terrible song
that turns the seasons.
And the earth, having its fill of light,
turned again toward darkness.

Bones—A City Poem

forget the great blue heron flying low
    over the marsh, its footprints
    still fresh in the sand

forget the taste of wild mushrooms
    and where to find them

forget lichen-covered pines
    and iceland moss

forget the one-legged duck
    and the eggs of the snapping turtle
    laid in the bank

forget the frog found in the belly of a bass

forget the cove testing its breath
    against the autumn morning

forget the down-filled nest
    and the snake swimming at midday

forget the bullhead lilies
    and the whiskers
    of the pout

forget walking on black ice
    beneath the sky hunter's bow

forget the living waters
    of Quinsigamond

forget how to find the Pole star and why

forget the eyes of the red fox
    the hornets that made their home
    in the skull of a cow

forget waking to hear the call of the loon

forget that raccoons are younger brothers
    to the bear

forget that you are walking
    on the bones of your grandmothers

Blessings

—for Renée

Under the raspberry bushes is a place of cool grass and quiet. The sun comes in through the spaces between the leaves, but no-one can see me as I sit here. Someone walks by on the path, I can see their sneakers and tanned legs, knees at my eye level. I am very still and they don't know I'm here. After a while the birds accept my presence and start to chirp to each other and land on the berry bushes. I, like them, want to taste the juicy ripe redness, so sweet and warm in the sun. When I reach up to pluck the red berries, they fall into my hand.

*　　*　　*　　*

One day between the corn and Mr. Phillips deserted pig barn, I find a flower taller than my father. It is a brown-eyed susan, I think, a flower I know well, only somehow grown large, its center flattened and whorled. I look around to see if other flowers are following this one's lead, or if I am getting smaller, but no, they are all their usual size, only this giant face turned toward the sun, yellow petals flung back, the familiar hairy stalk thick as my arm. I stare in silence for awhile, then go inside to find my Memere. I tug on her arm. I have no words to explain what I have seen, she will not believe it, I'm sure, so all I can do is pull her outside. *Come and see.* She follows me up the path, and there it is, leaning toward the sun. We stand for a moment amid the droning of bees, the wind soft on our faces, the timothy brushing around our legs and ankles. *Well, that's really something,* she says finally. She doesn't name it, but leaves the mystery, and each day I return, in awe of miracles, to view this magic blossom, this petaled face, this flower of sun.

*　　*　　*　　*

Each day we come here. To this tree that holds water in its arm, like a mother holding the head of her baby. Some days she offers us water from a bowl held in the palm of her upturned hand. Other days, we find a font, like the one at church, except this one is our size, we don't need to stand on tiptoe to reach in over the edge. We can look into the dark water, see the bark edged deep green around the tiny pool, dip our whole hand in if we want to. But we don't want to. It is just the tips of our fingers that brush the water gently, and we touch our foreheads, breasts and shoulders. Though no one tells us to, we leave behind a pile of carefully selected acorns, a yellow leaf, a pussywillow wand. Each day we come here. Each day we receive the blessing.

The Sweet and Vinegary Taste

—for my grandmother, Rose LeBlanc Meunier

Summer overflowed the kitchen
where Memere made pepper relish
and piccalilli,
cooked up tons of beans,
and served us cucumbers and tomatoes
three times a day.

Every morning I followed her
down the cellar stairs
and out the back door
a load of laundry in her arms,
a bag of clothespins in mine.

A big girl now,
I grabbed the pole
and lowered the clothesline.
I hung the little things,
socks, underwear,
while Memere hung the sheets.

The line heavy with clothes,
Memere helped me push the pole
until the sheets swung
above my head,
closer to the wind, Memere said,
and safe from dogs.

But laundry was just an excuse.
The garden was what pulled us out,
and after clothes were hung
we walked our usual path
in and out among the beans and squash,
pulling a weed here, flicking a caterpillar
from the tender vines.
We buried fish
to make the plants grow.
We tied tin pie plates to strings

to keep the birds away, and
Memere wasn't bothered if
it didn't work. Birds flew
above and walked through the corn.
When I raised my arms and ran
to chase them Memere's voice would come,
Bury the fish, she said, and let the birds be.

Her knobby hands
working in the dark brown
New England soil
never seemed to doubt
there'd be enough.
This piece of earth
we called garden
was home, she knew,
to many, and not ours alone.

Bury the fish and let the birds be,
she said. There will be enough.

And there was enough.
Enough for everybody,
for birds, and rabbits,
and caterpillars, enough
and more than enough
to overflow the kitchen,
to fill the winter shelves
with the sweet and vinegary taste
of life, the mystery
flowing from the earth
through her hands
to our open mouths.

Too'kay

This is the pie
that defines our Frenchness
in the winter season

the Christmas Eve pie
of twice ground pork
cooked slowly
seasoned lightly with salt and pepper

we make dozens to give away
but Uncle Raymond won't eat our pie
missing the spices his tongue demands

he calls it *tourtiere*
says there's no such thing as *too'kay*

but there it is
written in Memere's book
the Indian *k* replacing the *r*
as foreign to Algonkin tongues

as the spices
Memere leaves out

After Hours

After hours at the hospital
my grandmother is baking pies,
Christmas turkeys, and hams
for the doctors whose wives are home
sipping eggnog around the fireplace,
or out at parties, their shoulders bare and elegant.

No one bakes a pie like you, Rose,
the doctors say. She is proud of her baking,
proud to cook for these doctors,
and doesn't charge them for her time,
but accepts the money they press on her
as gifts. They are equals in this
Christmas giving.

I want to take her home.
I want to get her out of that kitchen,
where outside I know the old chevy waits,
her son-in-law, my father, at the wheel,
her youngest daughter waving
and the faces of five of her grandchildren
pressed to the glass. That is me, the oldest one
of this batch, sent in to call her home.

But I can't call her out of that kitchen.
She is there, she is still there,
baking, cooking, cleaning ovens,
she is 68, she is 69, she is 70 years old.

I want to hold her hands,
I want to take her hands
and coax her outside
where by now the car door has fallen open,
and the children are calling to her
in the voices of young birds.

Memere, it is Christmas again,
and I know you are working somewhere.
If I could find you I would give you my hand.
I want us to be traveling together,
your body warm cinnamon
in the snowy night.

Comes Down Like Milk

My mother's curls
have come undone.
She washes her mother's legs
and covers them
in clean sheets.
When we lean over
to turn her shrunken body
Memere takes a sharp breath.
My mother and I become still,
our bodies grow bigger
trying to absorb the pain.

We wait for the soft moan.
Instead, Memere grasps
the braid running down my back.

While I adjust the pillow,
my mother gets comb and brush.
Together we take out the pins.
Memere's hair comes down like milk.

Night

—for Bill

We have stolen
the orange harvest moon
to light our fire
now she glows
chill silver.
Leaves fall on you
as you sleep.
Your eyes move beneath
their lids chasing
images I cannot
see. I had hoped to
keep you to myself
this night. The wind
pulls the smoke into
itself. Flames curl
securely around the logs.
I watch you sleep
your heavy length against
the ground. I want
to curl my warmth
around you, you
who dream through wind
and applesmoke.

Menora

—for Bill

Now after 20 years
he buys a menora
in the form of a bird

Not a Jew
I stand with him
and light the candles
each feather tipped with flame

Not Indian
he dances with me
at Pow Wows
breathes in the smoke of sage
lifts his face open to the sky

Mother Night: Full Moon Past Solstice

—for Doris

Tonight you lie on your side
extending your black body
past all seeing
and the earth, just one
in a litter of planets,
turns toward you,
and you bare your breast
to the winter night.

          Look, my husband says,
            there's a ring around the moon.

But no moon ring
ever filled my eyes like this,
from horizon to horizon,
and I press my face
against the night
and curl my fingers
into clouds
as I breathe in the cold winter sky
and wrap my lips around the moon.
What I taste are sweet
stars that fly spinning
and sparking against my teeth.
Soon entire galaxies
are flying down my throat
until the whole night is whirling
and pulsing inside me and I pull back
satisfied and smile,
thank you, Mother,

          Ice crystals, he explains,
          Yes, I say

and lick the stars from my lips.

Genealogy

Grandma was born
on two different days
and on her birth and death
certificates her mother's name
is not the same

Her maiden name
she always told me was
Laforte, the strong,
but now I find it is Lafford,
as in a place to cross rivers
as in having to pay the price
of crossing

Roseanna

it is presented to me this way
poor immigrant woman
washing floors in payment
on a dream

but she is not immigrant
though her family has moved twice
pushed out by the English
moved west, vanished

She is washing the floors
in the school where her children are kept
her husband gone following work
her skin too dark to rescue them

she follows the grain of wood
with her eyes, her hands
moving in circles, the water
sloshing over knuckles

cracked with harsh soap
and cold. She follows
the grain of wood
in which she can see the hearts

of her children,
see how this one's laughter ends here
where two boards meet, where this one's breath
gets caught, where the light in this one's eyes

recedes into shadow. When her husband returns
they will go together and claim the children
they will leave this place
crossing borders and languages

they will take on the mask of immigrant
their children safely home
not watching from a window
for a glimpse of her remembered face

After Listening to a Reading of Romantic Poems About Columbus: One More Thought

His name
was my grandmother's
favorite curse word

Survival

On Cape Cod
the colonists bring their
animals tied to the yoke
and plow the mother's breast
planting in long rows,
separating one crop
from the other

the corn's feet grow cold
the harvest small, and eaten
by raccoons who raid nightly
with no squash bristles
to threaten their delicate feet

In winter, angry winds
carry the earth
someplace else
til there is nothing left
but this sand
where white pine,
shrunk from grandfather forests
to these survivors,
hold hands across the dunes

I know that inside the white pine
there is food to survive a winter
that the wide plantain leaves
pushing up through the old driveway
could make a salad, that the furry berries
of the staghorn sumac will make
a winter tea for me, and be first food
to returning birds come spring

how much is forgotten?

the earth is cold now
but when the dogwood blossoms
it will be warm enough

to hold the seed corn
and coax it into growth

see how the hill catches the sun
for the young roots of corn
see how the corn stays the winter
holding the earth safe
through furious winds

Medicine Woman

—*for Dovie*

medicine woman they call me
as if I should like it
like the kids in school
who called me little white dove
from some stupid song
about one more Indian woman
jumping to her death
how come you have an animal name?
they asked me, how come?
and I went home to ask my father
how come, Dad, how come
I have an animal name?

now white women come into my shop
and ask me to bless their houses
(what's wrong with them, I want to ask)
name their grandchildren
(do I know your daughters?)
blow some smoke around
say some words, do
whatever it is you do
we want someone spiritual—
you're Indian, right?

right. my tongue is held
by their grey hair
they are grandmothers
deserving of respect
and so I speak
as gently as I can
you'd let me, a stranger,
come into your home, I ask
let me touch
your new grandchild
let me name
the baby
anything

that comes into my head?
I am not believing this
but they are smiling
and tell me again
we want someone
spiritual
to do it

I write to my father
how come you never
told me who we are, where
we came from?

Women keep coming into my shop
putting stones in my hands
Can you feel that? they ask
Of course I can feel it
I'm not dead, but that
is not the right answer

My father writes back
the garden is doing good
the corn is up
there's lots of butterflies
all I know is
we come from the stars.

To Human Skin

My father's eyes were blue
like his grandfather's
but if I trace the line
of nose and chin
it is his grandmother's face
I see. Abenaki woman.

His heart was green and growing,
as if he'd lived for centuries,
an old forest tree man
rooted in the rocky soil
now called new england,
as if Gluscabe's arrow
had just pierced the bark
and turned it to human skin.

Ndakinna, I want to tell him now.
Ndakinna. There is a name
for this place you call in English
the home country.

Over the last meal
we'll ever eat together
he tells me, I'm going up north,
up to the old home country,
Abenaki country. He smiles
in anticipation, his feet
already feeling the forest floor,
while my stomach tightens
with the knowledge that he
is going home. I push
the feeling away. But when spirit
talks to spirit, there is no denying.

Through the long days of mourning,
I see my father's spirit
walk into the bright autumn woods.
Red, gold, and evergreen,

they welcome him back,
his relatives, green of heart,
and rooted, like him,
in the soil of this land
called Ndakinna.

At the Pow Wow

my mother, red-haired,
who lived with my father
forty years,
who buried my grandparents,
whose skin was brown, she said,
from age,
watches the feathered dancers
and says, so that's
what real Indians look like.

I wrap the shawl around my shoulders,
and join the circle.

Like the Trails of Ndakinna

We're French and Indian like the war
my father said
they fought together
against the English
and although that's true enough
it's still a lie
French and Indian
still fighting in my blood

The Jesuit who traveled up the St. Lawrence
found the people there uncivilized
they will not beat their children
he wrote in his diary by candlelight
and the men listen too much
to their wives

You who taught me to see no borders
to know the northeast as one land
never heard the word Ndakinna
but translated without knowing it
our country, Abenaki country

Grandmothers and grandfathers
are roaming in my blood
walking the land of my body
like the trails of Ndakinna
from shore to forest

They are walking restlessly
chased by blue eyes and white skin
surviving underground
invisibility their best defense
Grandmothers, grandfathers,
your blood runs thin in me
I catch sight of you
sideways in a mirror
the lines of nose and chin
startle me, then sink
behind the enemy's colors

You are walking the trails
that declare this body
Abenaki land
and like the dream man
you are speaking my true name
Ndakinna

All Night She Dreams

All night she dreams
a panther, a white bear,
a wet moose.
When she wakes
she is on turtle's back.
She can feel the lumbering
movement beneath her.
Here she can talk to fire,
to stone, and people take
many shapes.
She knows that one day
her hips will grow heavy
as squash,
she will lie on the earth
and vines will grow
from her arms and legs,
milky kernels will form
on the ears of corn plants
growing skyward from her breasts.
Meanwhile, there is walking in balance,
there is clear thought,
and song
rising from her lips
like smoke, like mist,
like welcome clouds,
like some green and beautiful plant.

CHERYL SAVAGEAU has received Fellowships in Poetry from the National Endowment for the Arts and the Massachusetts Artists Foundation, and three residencies at the MacDowell Colony. Savageau received Mentor of the Year and Writer of the Year Awards from Wordcraft Circle of Native Writers and Storytellers, and the Skipping Stones Book Award for Exceptional Multicultural and Nature/Ecology books for her children's book, *Muskrat Will Be Swimming*, (reissued by Tilbury House, 2006) which was also named a Notable Children's Book by *Smithsonian Magazine*.

Savageau is also a textile artist. Her quilts were recently on display at the University of New Hampshire, Durham.

CURBSTONE PRESS, INC.

is a nonprofit publishing house dedicated to literature that reflects a commitment to social change, with an emphasis on contemporary writing from Latino, Latin American and Vietnamese cultures. Curbstone presents writers who give voice to the unheard in a language that goes beyond denunciation to celebrate, honor and teach. Curbstone builds bridges between its writers and the public – from inner-city to rural areas, colleges to community centers, children to adults. Curbstone seeks out the highest aesthetic expression of the dedication to human rights and intercultural understanding: poetry, testimonies, novels, stories, and children's books.

This mission requires more than just producing books. It requires ensuring that as many people as possible learn about these books and read them. To achieve this, a large portion of Curbstone's schedule is dedicated to arranging tours and programs for its authors, working with public school and university teachers to enrich curricula, reaching out to underserved audiences by donating books and conducting readings and community programs, and promoting discussion in the media. It is only through these combined efforts that literature can truly make a difference.

Curbstone Press, like all nonprofit presses, depends on the support of individuals, foundations, and government agencies to bring you, the reader, works of literary merit and social significance which might not find a place in profit-driven publishing channels, and to bring the authors and their books into communities across the country. Our sincere thanks to the many individuals, foundations, and government agencies who have recently supported this endeavor: Community Foundation of Northeast Connecticut, Connecticut Commission on Culture & Tourism, Connecticut Humanities Council, Greater Hartford Arts Council, Hartford Courant Foundation, Lannan Foundation, National Endowment for the Arts, and the United Way of the Capital Area.

Please help to support Curbstone's efforts to present the diverse voices and views that make our culture richer. Tax-deductible donations can be made by check or credit card to:
Curbstone Press, 321 Jackson Street, Willimantic, CT 06226
phone: (860) 423-5110   fax: (860) 423-9242
www.curbstone.org